SMOKE

FREE

CONDOS

SMOKE FREE CONDOS

How We Restricted Smoking Inside Condominium Association Units and Declared Secondhand Smoke a Nuisance.

The "Gold Standard" Step-by-Step Guide

Dr. Joyce Starr

STARR PUBLISHING

Published by Starr Publishing | StarrPublishing.com | 786-693-4223

Cover Design © Starr Publishing, 2013. All Rights Reserved.

Second Edition: ISBN: 9798705612611,

Publishing Date: February 2021

First Edition: September 2013

ISBN 13: 978-0-9882394-7-0

ISBN 10: 0988239477

LCCN: 2013915967

Published in the United States of America

DISCLAIMER

This publication is intended to provide helpful and informative material. It is not intended to replace the advice of an attorney. No action should be taken solely on the contents of this book. Consult your association attorney before adopting any suggestions in this book or drawing inferences from it.

The author and publisher specifically disclaim all responsibility for any liability, loss or risk, personal or otherwise, which is incurred as a consequence, directly or indirectly, from the use or application of any contents in this book.

CONTENTS

I always wondered why somebody doesn't

do something about that.

Then I realized I was somebody.

Lily Tomlin

There are no shortcuts

to any place worth going.

Beverly Sills

SMOKING AND SECONDHAND SMOKE

RESTRICTIONS AMENDMENT

We took a stand against smoking and secondhand smoke. On October 1, 2012, our South Florida condominium association ("Association") voted to amend our Governing Declaration to restrict smoking within units and to declare secondhand smoke a nuisance.

Smoking in common areas—such as the pool and fire escapes—was also declared a violation. The only two exceptions are unit balconies—considered "limited" common areas—and the common area parking lot.

According to the Bureau of Tobacco Free Florida of the Florida Department of Health, we were—to the best of their knowledge—the first Florida condominium association to amend a Governing Declaration for this purpose.

Dr. Joyce Starr

This work details the political, procedural and legal hurdles that we encountered. Our experience will hopefully inspire community associations in Florida and across the nation to replicate our effort. The name of our condo is excluded for privacy reasons.

We did not seek publicity, nor did we publicize our victory at the time. Our singular focus was cleaner indoor air and a healthier quality of life for all residents. The change in our covenants, conditions and restrictions (CC&Rs) was filed with the county and state.

Several New York condominiums recently banned secondhand smoke. In the spring of 2013, the Zeckendorf Towers, a 670-unit mixed-use condominium at Union Square, became the largest condo complex in the country to put a smoke-free ban in place.

In the winter of 2012, One Grand Army Plaza, with ninety-eight units, restricted smoking in all common and limited common areas, except for private terraces and the roof. The Ariel West, a 32-story condo on the Upper West Side, banned smoking in 2011, charging a $150 fine for the first offense and an increase of $150 for each subsequent offense.

Utah prohibits smoking in all condominiums throughout the state. A number of California cities have also passed multifamily building smoking prohibitions.

In 2006, a Colorado court upheld an amendment to an association's Governing Declaration which banned smoking within the boundaries of condominium units. Comparing the smell of smoke to extremely loud noise that is not confined to a single area, thereby creating a nuisance to others, the court noted that the condo rules bar any nuisance that is a source of annoyance to residents. While not binding on other states, the Colorado case is an important precedent.

Apartment complexes are helping to create a smoke-free path. In June 2013, the Related Companies prohibited smoking in forty thousand rental units it owns or manages. "Although the program will roll out gradually, it appears to be the first of this scale by a national property owner," wrote C. J. Hughes in the *New York Times*, June 13, 2013.

Smoking restrictions on condo units are more difficult to achieve because they generally require a change in the bylaws. In our case, this required approval by two-thirds of the members, a nearly insurmountable percentage for a medium-sized or larger complex.

The Bureau of Tobacco Free Florida urges Florida condominiums and multi-unit housing properties to go smoke free, providing extensive education on the health impact of both secondhand and thirdhand smoke.

Thirdhand smoke is a toxic residue that clings to walls, carpets, clothes, cars and other surfaces long after secondhand smoke has dissipated.

The Lawrence Berkeley National Laboratory reported in June 2013 issue of *Metagenesis* that thirdhand smoke causes significant genetic damage in human cells. Berkeley Lab, with thirteen Nobel Prizes, is supported by the U.S. Department of Energy and is managed by the University of California (UC).

Their study found that "chronic exposure is worse than acute exposure, with the chemical compounds in samples exposed to chronic thirdhand smoke existing in higher concentrations and causing more DNA damage than samples exposed to acute thirdhand smoke, suggesting that the residue becomes more harmful over time."

According to Lara Gundel, a Berkeley Lab scientist and co-author of the study, "Tobacco-specific nitrosamines, some of the chemical compounds in thirdhand smoke, are among the most potent carcinogens there are. They stay on surfaces, and when those surfaces are clothing or carpets, the danger to children is especially serious."

Dr. Joyce Starr

The Berkely Lab study demonstrated that thirdhand smoke can still be detected in dust and surfaces several months after smokers move out. Vacuuming rugs or wiping down walls does not eliminate nicotine contamination. Instead, the materials become more toxic with the passage of time.

"You can do some things to reduce the odors, but it's very difficult to really clean it completely," said study co-author, Hugo Destaillats. "The best solution is to substitute materials, such as change the carpet, repaint."

Condominium common area hallway carpets and walls are seldom replaced or painted for decades, let alone to eliminate nicotine contamination.

MISSION

Our goal was to protect the health of our residents from excessive cigarette smoke that had been filtering through our air conditioning system, walls and corridors for years—primarily from one renter, but also from several unit owners.

Fortunately, vociferous and mounting complaints against the renter ultimately forged the consensus and motivation required for decisive action.

Efforts to convince the renter to smoke on his balcony with the sliding doors and interior windows closed had failed. Secondhand smoke filtered through his kitchen wall into an adjoining unit, destroying the owner's quiet enjoyment of property. Her kitchen cabinets, drawers and dishwasher reeked of stale smoke.

The renter's secondhand smoke toxins also blanketed the common area corridor whenever he opened his door. Even with the door closed, the disgusting smell reached the elevator about twenty feet away.

Amending the Governing Documents on such a highly charged issue requires leadership. Ideally, a Board officer should confer with the attorney on language and procedures—and also oversee the property manager in carrying out the process. Failure to do so can result in major delays and missteps.

One or more Board members and/or unit owners must be willing to actively encourage owners to cast a positive vote. Our initial Special Membership Meeting netted slightly over half the ballots required for passage and an insufficient number for a quorum. The session was called to order and immediately adjourned.

By law—if we wanted to count the first set of proxies in the final tally—we only had ninety days from the date of the first mailing to send out another mailing and to conduct a second Special Membership Meeting.

Garnering double the number of votes in ninety days required intense effort.

I took the lead in moving the amendment through the birthing process. My advice for others who want to do the same: Remain focused on the larger goal. You are bound to face opposition, even from board members and residents who detest secondhand smoke.

It was an uphill fight until the very last vote was counted, with a colorful cast of proponents, doubters and vigorous opponents. Shouting matches laced our condo meetings.

The owner of the unit threatened to sue if we attempted to restrict his renter from smoking inside his unit. He repeatedly emailed owners, urging them to join a lawsuit against the Association. We refused to back down, and his lawsuit failed to materialize.

Five months after passage—four years to the month that smoker/renter moved in—the owner finally agreed *in writing* that he would no longer allow smoking inside his unit. Further, according to our Addendum to Lease—which both the renter and owner signed—the owner must evict the renter and assume the eviction costs if his tenant violates our Documents in the future, including the new amendment.

A decision to evict cannot be based on frivolous or minor violations of the Documents. Violations by renters leading to eviction are conditioned on the following:

- Complaints by unit owners;

- Documentation by security and/or the property manager;

- Review by our Covenant Enforcement Committee; and

- A majority Board vote.

THE AMENDMENT PROCESS

Amending the Governing Declaration of a condo or homeowners association (HOA) is challenging under the best of circumstances. Typically, the Board proposes and votes for an amendment before presenting it to unit owners for their vote.

Association members must then be given an opportunity to vote by proxy for or against the amendment by a specific date, or to do so in person at the Special Membership Meeting held on that date.

Under our Documents, unit owners can also present an amendment for Board approval, so long as they convene a Special Membership Meeting and have the requisite number of votes to pass it. However, even if the Board approves a member initiated amendment, it must still be put to a general vote by all unit owners.

The vote must be conducted according to procedures specified in your Documents and also by state law, if applicable. The percentage of affirmative votes required to amend the bylaws should be found in your Documents.

Owners must be convinced to vote and to submit their proxy. (Negative votes count towards establishing the necessary quorum. Abstentions do not.)

Unfortunately, many ignore Association mail. Additional measures must be undertaken, including door-to-door visits, phone calls, elevator and lobby conversations—whatever is required. Hopefully, a group of unit owners will step up to the task.

In our condo, the majority of owners are employed, have young children, are elderly/not well, or do not have the time for or interest in greater involvement. Two women agreed to help. They went door-to-door for several days with proxies in hand. Even with repeat visits, they rarely found people at home and/or willing to open the door. It was very discouraging.

Our Board president was stridently opposed to the Smoking and Secondhand Smoke Restrictions Amendment and even convinced several owners to change their affirmative votes to no. (In the end, the president quietly voted *for* the Amendment.)

While other Board members supported the Amendment, none were willing to make a call, knock on a door or follow-up in any—due to shyness, work and travel schedules, or to the view that the Board should not actively lobby for passage.

Many believe that the property manager should take control. Do not place the burden of success on the property manager's shoulders. The manager cannot be expected to provide guidance to the Association attorney on amendment language, draft the perfect cover letter to residents, anticipate challenges, carry out the process and convince owners to vote. Someone, preferably a board member, must assume oversight responsibility and take the necessary actions to ensure success.

My recommendation: Educate yourself on amendment procedures. Obtain attorney input on key dates, the amendment package and the cover letter.

To her credit, our property manager handled mailings and meetings with precision. She spent considerable time explaining the purpose and value of the amendment to owners who visited her office or phoned for clarification. She also explained how to fill out a proxy and the importance of voting certificates.

If owners do not understand how to fill out a proxy form and/or fail to return their voting certificate, the amendment could fail—even if with the requisite number of votes.

For example, our proxy required that the proxy holder's name be entered on a line at the top of the form. The line can also be left empty, in which case it reverts to the secretary of the Association.

But a number of people did not understand or simply forgot and wrote their own name on the line for the proxy holder. We had received nearly a dozen yes votes with this error when we realized the potential mistake. I suggested that we seek the advice of our Association attorney.

A board officer insisted that we ignore the problem. "What if owners refuse to resubmit? Who will know the difference? What does it matter?"

Unwilling to take the risk, I sent our attorney an email explaining the issue. He insisted—in no uncertain terms—that we redo those proxies!

Lesson learned: We should have included three short sentences below the proxy holder's name: "Please do not write your name on this line! Insert the name of your *proxy holder*. If you leave the line blank, the Secretary of the Board will be your proxy holder."

The good news: All owners we approached patiently agreed to resubmit their forms. Imagine if we took the proposed shortcut (did nothing), and the votes were later challenged!

Dr. Joyce Starr

Amendments seldom pass without education. If you (or others) are unable or unwilling to educate fellow owners on the importance of the amendment, do not start the process.

If board members and/or management cannot be bothered with proper procedures, do not start the process.

But if you are ready to commit the time and energy—and to confront/absorb the stress—the results could be lifesaving.

NUISANCE

Nuisance is one of the oldest causes of action known to the common law, with cases framed in nuisance going back almost to the beginning of recorded case law. Nuisance signifies that the "right of quiet enjoyment" is being disrupted to such a degree that a tort is being committed.

en.wikipedia.org/wiki/nuisance

QUIET ENJOYMENT

The right of a property owner or tenant to enjoy his or her property without interference. Disruption of quiet enjoyment may constitute a legal nuisance. Leases and rental agreements often contain a "covenant of quiet enjoyment," expressly obligating the landlord to ensure that tenants live undisturbed.

nolo.com/dictionary/quiet-enjoyment-term.html

THE LAW OF NUISANCE

Governing documents of a condominium usually contain language such as the following: "The unit owner shall not permit or suffer anything to be done or kept in his unit which will increase the rate of insurance in the Condominium property, or which will obstruct or interfere with the rights of other unit owners or annoy them by unreasonable noises, or otherwise, nor shall the unit owners commit or permit any nuisance, immoral or illegal acts in or about the Condominium property."

The law of nuisance is grounded on the fundamental rule that every person should so use his own property as not to injure that of another.

Anything which annoys or disturbs one in the free use, possession, or enjoyment of his property, or which renders its ordinary use or occupation physically uncomfortable is a nuisance and may be restrained—Jones v. Trawick 75 So.2d 785. 787 (Fla. 1954). A nuisance is established when the property owner's use of his/her property results in injury to the legal rights of the complaining party—Beckman v. Marshall. 85 So.2d 552. 555 (Fla. 1956).

Not all use of one's property which annoys or disturbs a neighbor's enjoyment of property is prohibited. The issue is whether there is an appreciable, substantial, tangible injury resulting in actual, material, physical discomfort.

Discussing the 2006 Pompano Beach Florida case of Merrill vs. Bosser, Florida condo attorney Gary A. Poliakoff—Becker & Poliakoff—wrote in his firm's public newsletter on May 8, 2006:

"Eventually the non-smoking family sued the smoker under theories of trespass, common law nuisance, and breach of covenant [the declaration of condominium contains a provision which states, 'unit owner shall not permit or suffer anything to be done in his unit which will interfere with the right of another unit owner or annoy them by unreasonable noises, or otherwise, nor shall the unit owners commit or permit any nuisance in or about the condominium property.'

"The trial judge found that though there was no case on point in Florida which addressed whether secondhand smoke is considered a form of trespass onto real property, the unique facts of this case justified the finding that it does.

"In addition, the court, citing the authority of Florida's Supreme Court...held that anything which annoys or disturbs one in the free use, possession or enjoyment of his property, or which renders its ordinary use or occupancy physically uncomfortable, may become a nuisance.

"While a trial decision lacks precedential value, I am of the opinion that this well reasoned opinion will find its way into the precedents of Florida law." – Becker-Poliakoff.com

Florida attorney Gregory Eisinger – Eisinger, Brown, Lewis Frankel & Chaiet, P.A. – previously wrote a law review article in which he referenced statutory law and judicial decisions from Florida, as well as from other jurisdictions, relating to both nuisance issues and secondhand smoke (through 2011). His commentary included the following:

"Courts throughout the country have rendered opinions on what constitutes a private nuisance. One Florida court stated: 'This court recognizes that the law of private nuisance is bottomed on the fundamental rule that every person should so use his own property as not to injure that of another....Anything which annoys or disturbs one in the free use, possession, or enjoyment of his property, or which renders its ordinary use or occupation physically uncomfortable, is a 'nuisance' and may be restrained.'

"Other states have generally held similar definitions for the terms nuisance and private nuisance. A Nebraska Court of Appeals ruled that interference with the enjoyment of one's home by smoke, odor and similar attacks upon one's senses is a serious harm. A California trial court in Babbitt v. Superior Court stated that 'intrusions by smoke and noxious odors are traditionally appropriate subjects of nuisance actions,' and found that secondhand smoke from a cigar could constitute a nuisance.

"In Utah, secondhand smoke is unambiguously listed as a nuisance by statute. The statute defines a nuisance as 'anything which is injurious to health, indecent, offensive to the senses, or an obstruction to the free use of property so as to interfere with the comfortable enjoyment of life or property.'

"This statute includes tobacco smoke which makes its way into a condominium 'more than once in each of two or more consecutive seven-day periods.' There are also several federal and state laws which condominium owners may rely on when making a claim. One city in California has even taken the initiative to pass an ordinance banning smoking within multifamily residential units." —"Smoking in Residential Condominiums: Why Florida Should Take a Stand Against This Deadly Nuisance!"

Dr. Joyce Starr

Declares the law firm's co-founder and senior partner, Dennis Eisinger: "We are on a crusade to help eradicate the harmful effects of secondhand smoke in residential communities in Florida." And Mr. Eisinger, in his capacity as a principal in the development of a luxury condominium project in Fort Lauderdale known as AquaVita Las Olas, has mandated that the project's condominium documents strictly prohibit smoking in ALL condominium units and most common areas within the building.

This documentation provision appears to make AquaVita the first residential Condominium in South Florida to include smoke-free language in its original Governing Declaration. Mr. Eisinger believes that, in addition to creating a healthier environment for the community, most condominium buyers are more interested in, and will even pay a premium, to live in a community which is totally smoke free.

Why Not Just Sue?

By suing another condo owner or his chain-smoking tenant directly, a non-smoking condo owner lets her/his condo board off the legal hook. It's also an uncertain, expensive and lengthy journey. So why not just sue the association?

In most circumstances, a board is required by applicable law and by the condo association documents to protect and enforce quiet enjoyment of property. However, by suing the board, you will be suing yourself and fellow unit owners—since the board will use *your* condo fees to pay *their* attorney, while you sink deeper into debt.

The board could also threaten to levy a special assessment to fund the case, a sure fire method to convince fellow owners that you are a menace to the community. Indeed, they might not have a choice.

Dr. Joyce Starr

Travelers Casualty and Surety Company of America ("Travelers"), for example, includes a exclusion clause in their non-profit policies "based upon, arising out of, directly or indirectly resulting from, in consequence of, or in any way involving the actual, alleged or threatened discharge, release, escape or disposal of pollutants into or on real or personal property, water or the atmosphere."

Their definition of pollutants is all encompassing. "Pollutants means any substance located anywhere in the world exhibiting any hazardous characteristics as defined by or identified on a list of hazardous substances issued by the United States Environmental Protection Agency or a state, county, municipality or locality counterpart thereof. Such substances shall include, but not be limited to, solids, liquids, gaseous or thermal irritants, contaminants or smoke, vapor, soot, fumes, acids, alkalis, chemicals or waste materials. Pollutants shall also mean any other air emissions, odor, waste water, oil or oil products, infectious or medical waste, asbestos or asbestos products, electric or magnetic or electromagnetic fields and any noise."

However, once an association amends the Declaration to restrict smoking inside units and to define secondhand smoke as a nuisance, it could be argued that the dispute is not about a pollutant, per se, but instead about a violation of the Declaration. Please consult with your insurance agent and with your association attorney on this matter!

According to Andrew Spargo, Executive Vice President of Smith Watson Parker Insurance, insurance carriers might in the future provide discounts to condominiums and apartment buildings that have adopted smoke-free policies. In fact, the Bureau of Tobacco Free Florida of the Florida Department of Health is urging Florida carriers to do so.

Condo board members are also generally protected by insurance policies that indemnify individual board members—hold them harmless—for normal business judgments. Board members will argue that it was in the best financial interests of the association to avoid a costly legal battle with an owner and/or tenant over secondhand smoke violations. You will also have a difficult time proving that board officers intentionally subjected you to secondhand smoke.

The bottom line: Amending the Governing Declaration is a cakewalk compared to suing your association.

Daunting Odds

We needed 102 affirmative votes to pass the amendment, out of a total of 144 units. Our Declaration required seventy-five percent (75%) approval to change our bylaws, excluding those who lost voting rights due to a ninety-day failure to pay dues and/or assessment fees. In our case, eight owners were ineligible to vote.

Due to high threshold, our Declaration had not been amended since the building was constructed in the mid-1970s!

Naysayers warned that we would fail in the best of times, let alone during a difficult economy. Opponents stated with absolute certainty that we would be sued and lose. They raised a specter of staggering legal costs that would sink the Association.

Defending their castle, opponents compared secondhand smoke fumes to the smell of garlic and argued that restricting smoking inside units was akin to prohibiting sex. Remaining on course was exhausting.

However, in my view, there was no choice. The amendment was truly a matter of life, death, illness—and the loss of quality of life—for residents exposed daily to the egregious amount of secondhand smoke streaming through our building.

PRESENTING YOUR CASE

My first-hand experience with secondhand smoke began in October 2008, when the renter/heavy smoker moved in next door.

Subsequent years were acutely stressful, as documented in my book, *Secondhand Smoke Crimes: When Neighbors Poison You*. The work presented health and legal arguments against secondhand smoke in condominiums and multifamily housing.

Along with a neighbor on the same floor, I wrote numerous complaints and repeatedly petitioned the Board to take action against the smoker.

In 2009, our property manager wrote to the owner stating that the renter's lease would not be renewed. Unfortunately, the property manager was later reversed by the Board president mentioned above.

Dr. Joyce Starr

In 2010, the manager raised the matter with our Covenant Enforcement Committee. A fine was levied, but later lifted when the owner complained that his warped front door was to blame for his tenant's smoke entering the corridor. The Board president allowed the owner and renter to renew their lease for another two-year period.

Since our Documents did not define secondhand smoke as a nuisance, board members refused to challenge the president—fearing a costly eviction process, the risk of a lawsuit by the owner, and the president's strident position.

Unfortunately, the renter continued to smoke like a human chimney inside his unit. The smell was unbearable. By the time we passed the Secondhand Smoke Amendment, there were over two hundred complaints against him, including:

"The smoke is filling my kitchen, foyer and all drawers and cabinets in my kitchen. I have been living with it for years. PLEASE do something!"

"I am writing to report yet another incident of secondhand smoke. *Where*: I suffered the stale smell of secondhand smoke in my kitchen and living room. *How bad*: On a scale of one to ten, it was the worst at ten. Request: My right to peaceful enjoyment of property has again been violated. Please take action against the smoker. "

When all else failed, I requested the opportunity to speak at Board meetings on the health dangers of secondhand smoke, as well as legal precedents across the nation. I made my requests in writing, asking for the full three minutes allotted to those who petitioned the Board in advance.

Dr. Joyce Starr

While the manager granted my request on several occasions, these were hardly uplifting experiences. I was heckled and booed by a handful of unit owners. When I referred to reports and warnings on secondhand smoke from the Surgeon General of the United States, I was met with blank stares. Those from other countries, including several Board members, had no idea who I was talking about.

One owner/smoker called me the "worst human being he had ever met" and, with great fanfare, ran out of the club room, slamming the door behind him, while others clapped. I asked an elderly Board member—whom I considered a friend—why she joined the chorus. "I don't really know," she replied. "Others were clapping, so I joined in."

If I took the negative reaction to heart, and let it stop me, the smoke-free effort would have died an early death. In the condo world, people are against you today, for you tomorrow, but may not recall the reason for either sentiment a week later. There is nearly universal fear that smoking restrictions will result in lawsuits, higher condo fees and constrain the ability to sell or rent a unit.

Opponents will play on that fear, justified or not. A smoke-free environment is more likely to reduce maintenance and replacements costs, while attracting buyers/renters at a higher price.

A reader of *Secondhand Smoke Crimes* wrote, "Just tell me what to do." If I were to advise her to be prepared for a multi-year battle, to research every nook and cranny, to make the case at repeated Board meetings, and to run for the Board, would she do it?

Ron Davis, Statewide Tobacco Policy Manager for smoke-free multi-unit housing (Bureau of Tobacco Free Florida, Florida Department of Health), counsels, "Know your board. Those decision makers are key. Smoke-free proponents need to understand what motivates them.

Dr. Joyce Starr

"Some are primarily concerned about the bottom line, while others care more about health issues. Tailor your argument to their motivations. Approach them individually. Natural allies may not be obvious at the beginning."

I won't promise you an easy road to victory, but I can assure you that it's possible. As Ron Davis advises, "Be ready to stand up to attacks. People on both sides feel passionate about this issue. The opposition can be fierce."

My speaking efforts seemed to fall on deaf ears, but in fact, the information imparted was slowly changing minds and hearts.

CONDO BOARD PASSES AMENDMENT

Miraculously, at the final Board meeting in 2011, a fierce Board challenger on the second smoke issue proposed amending our Documents to restrict smoking inside our units!

I was addressing the Board when he suddenly interjected: "I motion to direct our attorney to prepare language to amend our Documents on secondhand smoke."

We could barely hear him over the screams comparing restrictions on secondhand smoke to a ban on Indian food, Italian cuisine and bacon. It was near bedlam when he made his motion. He was asked several times to repeat himself.

Fortunately, the stars were aligned. The adversarial president had resigned a few months earlier in the middle of her term. The remaining members voted in the affirmative.

Board adversaries might honestly disagree with your position. Perhaps their agenda is at risk, and you're in the way. They might not even be able to define why they're fighting you. Perhaps they don't like your attitude or even the way you dress.

When I later asked this Board member why he made the motion, he revealed that family and friends had died of lung cancer and specifically from exposure to secondhand smoke. He said that he disliked the smell of smoke almost as much as I did!

But then he added, "And if it fails, I'll get you off my back." He apparently believed that the chance of approval by Association members was slim to none. Regardless, his motion was the first step in final passage of the Secondhand Smoke Amendment. After years of arguing, the motion passed in nano-seconds.

Since this was the final Board meeting of the year, the precise language would be defined by our attorney in consultation with the incoming Board of 2012. Passing a motion, formalizing the language and getting the number of votes required are worlds apart.

Why not a simple rule change? Condo and HOA Boards can pass a rule without unit owner approval, while obtaining the requisite number of affirmative votes for an amendment is a daunting proposition.

The risk of failure in our case was considerable. Still, it was the right decision and worth the risk. Rule changes are more vulnerable to legal challenges, whereas Document amendments carry heavier legal weight.

According to a 2002 Florida Supreme Court ruling (Woodside Case), owner rights can be altered through "a validly enacted amendment."

> "Thus, we find that respondents were on notice that the unique form of ownership they acquired when they purchased their units in the Woodside Village Condominium was subject to change through the amendment process, and that they would be bound by properly adopted amendments."

Dr. Joyce Starr

—Woodside Village Condominium Association, Inc. v. Jahren, 806 So. 2d 452 (Fla. 2002).

INTERNAL BOARD POLITICS

Much to everyone's surprise, I was elected to the Board in the 2012 annual election and subsequently elected treasurer by my Board colleagues.

Through this strange turn of events, I was accorded the responsibility to work with our attorney on drafting the amendment, as well as to ensure passage of the unit owner vote.

While we all expected challenges to the amendment from several heavy smokers and from owners who rented their units, no one anticipated that our Board president would prove to be the greatest roadblock.

After resigning from the Board in mid-2011, she ran again in 2012 and, through clever "deal-making," was reelected president. What turned her against the amendment? Frankly, it was inexplicable and irrational.

She claimed that we would be sued by the tenant smoker and by the owner of the unit. She provided the owner with privileged Board information and even contacted our insurance carrier, warning them not to cover us in the event of a lawsuit.

She stomped up and down at meetings, asserting that we had already spent twice on the process than was actually the case. Pointing a bony finger in my face, she bellowed: "Why don't you move?!" It was one long crisis after another.

Condo board members are like a pot luck dinner—you never know what personality traits and problems people will bring to the table.

Survey Owners

Condo and HOA Boards propose amendments to their membership for a formal vote by mailing a notice of the special membership meeting, together with the amendment text and a limited proxy form.

However, associations might first conduct a survey to obtain the pulse of the community. A survey is voluntary and is not required to amend the declaration.

With a sensitive issue like smoking, it's an inexpensive way to gauge the interest and support of the membership prior to incurring the time and expense of a formal membership meeting and vote.

An accompanying cover letter should clarify intent of the survey, (i.e., to gauge the interest of the membership in amending the declaration). Once feedback is obtained, your Board will hopefully be in position to propose a formal vote

Dr. Joyce Starr

by sending the actual text of the proposed amendment, along with notice of a Special Membership Meeting and the Limited Proxy form.

In our case, the survey was unnecessary. After almost four years of vigorous debate and discussion, it was time to move forward. Those who objected had already done so loudly and fervently.

THE RIGHT ATTORNEY

Our attorney did an outstanding job. Potential mistakes and future challenges were avoided due to the language he crafted and to his overriding concern that the process be conducted according to the letter of the law.

If the language of your amendment has not been drafted by a qualified attorney, don't even start the process. Fearful of escalating attorney fees, condo and HOA members often underestimate the value of a proactive, knowledgeable attorney.

In my experience, the right attorney can save your association major expenses down the road. Our final costs were reasonable by any measure. Board members often assert that the attorney "is just doing the job he/she is paid to do." Words of appreciation might encourage the attorney to bill for extra time! I see it differently.

Dr. Joyce Starr

Moreover, Board members and managers often insist that they **know** how to conduct legal processes when they don't have a clue. I cannot tell you how often I heard Board members say, "This is the way it SHOULD be done. I KNOW!"

I wrote to our attorney, "I deeply appreciate your diligence and concern that we take the right steps. Thank you for the comprehensive explanation of issues that might arise. I apprised the Board; all are grateful that you saved us from mistakes that would have ruined the process. It's not the first time!

"Moving towards the finish line, we could not have reached this 'hopeful' point without your guidance and superb language. This complex process was conducted with flawless precision due to your involvement. "

Amendment Language

I asked our attorney if we could offer several alternatives to our unit owners. With two or three choices on the table, one was likely to pass. I presented him with three options:

1. Language declaring our Association smoke-free, by prohibiting smoking in the condominium units, balconies, the common and/or limited common elements of the condominium, the recreational facilities or any portion of the condominium property.

2. Language which prohibited smoking inside condominium units and all common and limited common elements of the Condominium, with the exception of unit owner balconies and the parking lot.

3. Language stating a preference for a smoke-free building, but restricting smoking to limited common area balconies.

He counseled that it is much better practice to propose one option to the membership for a straight "yes" or "no" vote.

The Board of 2012, which included Board members from 2011, selected the second option, concluding that the best chance for passage was to allow residents to smoke on their balconies with the sliding glass doors and interior windows closed.

Smoking would **not** be permitted in the swimming pool, nor in our recreation facilities. While our priority was to prohibit smoking inside units, we wanted to take it as far as possible.

We all preferred that the building be one hundred percent (100%) smoke free. However, if we over-reached and failed, all would be lost. There would be little incentive or will to assume the cost, risk and effort a second time.

At least thirty smokers resided in the complex. If the amendment banned smoking in all areas of a condominium, smoking would be prohibited outside the building as well. A parking lot ban could cost crucial votes.

Balcony smoke that flows into neighboring units *can* cause health problems and negatively affect quiet enjoyment of property.

Since few residents in our South Florida building keep their windows open, there is less likelihood that secondhand smoke will travel from a smoker's balcony into a nearby window. On the other hand, tens of thousands of condo owners across the country live in buildings where smoking is permitted on balconies, and where smoke fumes enter into adjacent units or those above/below.

The formal definition of secondhand smoke as a legal nuisance is a powerful weapon. While our residents are permitted to smoke on their balconies, it does not give them the right to destroy the quiet enjoyment of others or to create a nuisance. Those suffering excessive secondhand smoke from a neighboring balcony could, in principle, demand and receive protection.

I told our attorney, "If we can't pitch a perfect game, we can still win the series. The fight for our right to clean indoor air begins. "

The Amendment

The letter "B" below represents the name of the Association. The full name is included in the copy on file with the county and state.

SMOKING AND SECONDHAND SMOKE RESTRICTIONS AMENDMENT

From the effective date of this amendment, in consideration of the health and welfare of the residents of B... Condominium/Association, and the known health hazards of secondhand smoke, the following prohibitions and restrictions on smoking and secondhand smoke are hereby adopted and established for B... Condominium/Association. For purposes of this paragraph, "secondhand smoke" means smoke emitted from lighted, smoldering, or burning tobacco when the smoker is not inhaling: smoke emitted at the mouthpiece during puff drawing: and smoke exhaled by the smoker. For purposes of this paragraph, "smoking" means inhaling, exhaling. burning, carrying, or possessing any lighted tobacco product, including cigarettes, cigars. pipe tobacco, and any other lighted tobacco product. Smoking and secondhand smoke are hereby declared and deemed a nuisance as described in this Declaration, including, but not limited to, the description in Article XII of this Declaration of Condominium. It is further hereby declared that smoking and secondhand smoke obstructs and interferes with the rights of other unit owners/residents to the peaceful enjoyment of their Units. Accordingly, smoking in the Condominium Units, the Common and/or Limited Common Elements of the Condominium, the recreational facilities or any portion of the Condominium Property is hereby strictly prohibited. Notwithstanding the foregoing, the aforementioned prohibition on smoking does not apply to the individual Limited Common Element balconies/terraces where smoking shall be permitted, provided that balcony/terrace doors and internal windows must be kept completely closed when smoking on a balcony/terrace. In addition, smoking on the fire terraces is hereby strictly prohibited. In the event of a violation of this

Dr. Joyce Starr

paragraph by any unit owner, occupant, resident, lessee, guest or invitee, the Association, by direction of its Board of Directors, may exercise any and all rights and remedies available to it under its governing documents and/or Florida Statutes, as they may be amended from time to time including, but not limited to the levying of violation fines, an action for injunctive relief, etc.

Cover Letter + Enclosures

The amendment package might include a cover letter urging passage of the amendment, along with relevant background information.

The package <u>must</u> include the exact text of the proposed amendment language (drafted by a qualified attorney), a notice of the Special Membership Meeting at which the membership vote will be conducted, a limited proxy voting form and possibly a voting certificate form (if required by the association Documents).

If a cover letter is included, it should be signed by "The Board," the president or by a member of your Board. While your property manager can sign the cover letter, it will not carry the same weight.

Some might argue that the cover letter should only state the language of the Amendment, date, time and place. In my view, the letter should explain why a positive vote would be to the advantage of the entire community! After all, the Board is spending owner funds on the procedure.

You can't simply write, "Please attend a Special Membership Meeting on a new Amendment and vote yes or no." There has to be more to it.

To repeat, the enclosures must include:

- The exact text of the proposed amendment language

- A notice of a Special Membership Meeting at which the membership vote will be conducted;

- A limited proxy voting form and possibly a voting certificate form (if required by the association's Governing Documents).

Several owners asked, "Does this mean we can no longer rent our units to smokers?" According to our attorney, even if the amendment passed, our Association would not have a legal basis to reject smoker applicants, as they would still be permitted to smoke on their balconies. If the association ultimately amends its Declaration to prohibit smoking in all areas, thus becoming a true "smoke-free" building—and assuming that there are no future changes in the law regarding this issue—the association could have a legal basis to reject a smoker applicant. (Consult with your attorney.)

On the other hand, prospective owners and renters should be made aware of the amendment during screening sessions.

We have had a wonderful response to the Secondhand Smoke Amendment from renters who have since moved into the building. We inform them about the amendment during the screening interview. All have welcomed it as further reason why they want to live in our building. None are smokers.

Owners are happy about the quality of renters we are attracting and with our reputation as a health conscious building.

We are most likely to get angry and excited in our opposition to some idea when we ourselves are not quite certain of our own position, and we are inwardly tempted to take the other side.

Thomas Mann

Grain by Grain

The first mailing to members netted only fifty-eight affirmative proxy votes, along with several no votes.

As mentioned above, we had an insufficient number of proxies to constitute a quorum at the July 9, 2012 Special Membership Meeting. The session was therefore called to order, adjourned and rescheduled for October 1, 2012.

By law, we still had ninety days from the date of our first mailing to pass the amendment. As a friend described the process, it was like building a pyramid—one grain of sand at a time.

Having shepherded the Board through the legal hurdles—working with the attorney over several months on the precise language and procedures—the next stage was crucial: obtaining the necessary proxy votes and voting certificates.

Voting certificates are crucial. In several instances, ownership had long ago passed from parents to adult children, but the latter failed to update the unit owner record with the state.

Individuals or companies who own several units are required by law to have a voting certificate on file for each unit. Companies must list and include the signature of their president, which as we learned, is often difficult to obtain.

I made a half-dozen calls to one owner to obtain his voting certificate, which he repeatedly promised to send. He submitted the proxy early on, but we only received his voting certificate a day before the final vote. To phone or wait? Each call contained the risk of drawing ire from the other party.

By the end of July, I brought in another twenty votes by directly phoning, emailing and meeting with owners. Small as that number sounds, it was nearly a full time job. I hit the proverbial wall of concern. We had over thirty absentee owners, and I didn't know a single one.

How could I obtain the additional twenty-four votes needed, plus an extra four or five to ensure a safe margin? How could I convince owners based in

Latin America, Europe, Israel and elsewhere, especially if there was a language barrier?

That's when a hero appeared—one with true horsepower. First Service Residential Regional Director Anselmo "Mo" Liano—our property manager from 2006 to 2009—understood my distress and offered to help. (First Service Residential managed our property.)

We would not have succeeded without his intervention. The force of his gentle, persuasive personality in reaching out to owners across different time zones made all the difference. He also retained warm relationships with many owners from his days as our onsite manager.

Mo undertook countless telephone calls, along with follow-up emails and faxes. He placed most of the calls during dinner hours and weekends. He made a half-dozen follow-up calls to a single individual who owned multiple units, in order to obtain voting certificates for each unit.

Even though the owner supported our cause, he was protected by an administrative gate keeper who wouldn't or couldn't get it done. Mo wouldn't take "too busy" for an answer. The certificates arrived. We breathed easier.

We met weekly for several hours at a time. In many cases, I made the initial call and/or sent an email, while he followed up, bringing in the final vote. He brought in five votes on a single day on the eve of his vacation. Mo never once doubted the outcome.

He ensured that procedures were conducted with absolute transparency, that all proxies were properly documented and that any missing certificates were obtained. He also provided an updated proxy roster and final vote tally list.

Mo's astute approach to record keeping resulted in better management of an ever expanding set of files, while his insistence that we cross every "t" and dot every "I" kept us on the straight and narrow.

He was constantly "thinking forward" in order to avoid potential legal challenges, including those that might be waged and won on minute technicalities.

Mo's job description calls for supporting Board initiatives. But his character and heart transformed responsibility into victory. He took us across the finish line.

Gary Pyott, President South Florida, First Service Residential, fully supported Mo's proactive approach. In keeping with its reputation for environmental leadership, the company took a courageous stand on a provocative issue.

One hundred and eight owners voted for the Secondhand Smoke Amendment. Only eleven owners voted against it. You might call it a landslide, except that obtaining those precious votes was akin to mining for gold with a teaspoon of hope.

You may talk of the tyranny of Nero and Tiberius; but the real tyranny is the tyranny of your next-door neighbor.

Walter Bagehot

A bad neighbor is a misfortune, as much as a good one is a blessing.

Hesiod, 700 B.C.

TALLYING THE VOTES

admit that I was worried! Mo's previously scheduled vacation fell on the date of the final vote! Fortunately, his colleague, Regional Director George Barriere, agreed to chair the Special Membership Meeting in his absence.

On the assumption that everything that can go wrong usually does, our mutual goal was to anticipate and prevent the unforseen. A soft-spoken yet forceful individual, George commanded respect. Equally important, he had considerable experience in chairing vote tally meetings on Declaration amendments.

Calling the meeting to order, he immediately asked for volunteers to tally the votes. An individual strongly opposed to the amendment quickly raised his hand, and George selected him. It was the right decision.

Two unit owners tried to disrupt the session with negative comments. George made it clear that there would be no further debate. The purpose of the Special Membership Meeting was purely to count votes. To my relief, he quickly brought the meeting under control.

Our Board secretary reviewed and verified all proxies and voting certificates prior to the meeting, checking each name against the roster that Mo provided. The Board secretary should confirm that all names, proxies, and voting certificates are in order.

She also took meeting minutes, which she sent to our attorney. Minutes represent a vital record of such an event, including details required for filing an amendment with the county and state.

Special Credit to Owners

Special credit goes to all owners who took the time to vote, whether for or against, and especially those who made an exceptional effort to do so.

One elderly gentleman promised to vote for the Amendment, but passed away shortly before the paperwork arrived. His wife and daughter were so moved by our cause that they signed the proxy, as well as a revised voting certificate, as soon as their mourning period ended.

Overseas destinations worked against us. In several instances, our mailing didn't arrive, and we had to resend the proxy and voting certificate by email or fax. Our attorney advised that scanned and faxed copies were acceptable.

However, with the deadline fast approaching, return mailings were problematic. The majority of non-resident owners were willing to scan and email them back to us. A few sent them by fax. An elderly woman in Brazil, with limited computer skills and no fax machine, took the document to a local UPS store and asked that it be returned to us by fax. Unfortunately, she failed to include certain information.

We emailed another blank proxy and voting certificate to her attention at the UPS store. She sent the second version, but placed her name on the line for the proxy holder, thereby invalidating the proxy. After multiple phone calls and her third visit to UPS, we finally had the precious proxy and voting certificate in hand—language barriers overcome.

We were warned that owners living overseas would have little patience for the secondhand smoke issue. The exact opposite occurred. Owners residing in Israel, Europe and Latin America rallied behind the Amendment.

Prospective owners were immediately informed about the Amendment. Several stated that a smoke-free environment was the one of the primary attractions of our building.

COSTS AND CALCULATIONS

The cost of inaction far outweighs the expense of passing an amendment. As noted above, we were warned that the attempt to restrict smoking inside units would destroy our budget, result in a law suit and require an assessment.

Yet, we spent less than $35 per unit! The real cost was in time, effort and heart.

Amendment costs include attorney fees, mailings required by law and filing fees. We sent two mailings at a cost of roughly one thousand dollars. Attorney fees, filing fees and association goals vary by state, the number of units and goals.

The best way to reduce legal fees is to streamline communications with your association attorney. Do not expect your attorney to read the board's mind and/or to make decisions for the Association—especially on such a controversial matter.

Dr. Joyce Starr

He/she will want to research cases and state laws related to secondhand smoke. You could potentially reduce the time charged to your association by sharing a copy of this book.

Costs can be contained through a familiarity with procedures, meeting deadlines, avoidance of missteps, and the support of your neighbors.

CONCLUSION

There is no constitutional right to smoke in your condominium or HOA! State and county courts have been taking a more favorable view on legal challenges to secondhand smoke in condominiums, coops and apartment buildings.

As noted above, Utah and several California cities have legislated no-smoking policies for both condominiums and apartment buildings.

Even where state laws lag, state agencies like the Bureau of Tobacco Free Florida of the Florida Department of Health are spearheading proactive, educational initiatives at the local level. At least thirty Florida community associations were established at the outset as smoke-free zones.

The California Tobacco Control Program funds the American Lung Association Smokefree Housing Initiative and other community organizations that have played a key role in city-wide changes.

Dr. Joyce Starr

Organizations at the forefront of legislative developments include: the Smoke-Free Environments Law Project (SFELP) of Michigan; Americans for Nonsmokers Rights (ANR), headquartered in California with nationwide offices; Action on Smoking and Health (ASH), California-based and active on legislative issues; and the Group Against Smog & Pollution (GASP), with numerous US and UK chapters. Dedicated groups across the nation have provided invaluable legal, medical and scientific insight.

The California Consortium on the Health Effects of Thirdhand Smoke, established in 2011, is funded by the Tobacco-Related Disease Research Program—managed by the University of California and funded by state cigarette taxes.

In spite of formidable obstacles, condominium associations and HOAs can and will rally to ensure cleaner indoor air.

About the Author

Dr. Joyce Starr has authored 20+ books on wide-ranging topics. A condo/HOA rights expert, her works include: *Defend Your Condo & Homeowner Association Rights—What You Must Do When Your Condo Board Turns Your Life Upside Down;* and *Secondhand Smoke Abuse—When Neighbors Threaten Your Health, Children & Pets with Secondhand Smoke.* View our Condo & HOA series page on Amazon.com.

Board treasurer of her condominium in 2012, she guided the Smoking and Secondhand Smoke Restrictions Amendment through the approval process.

Dr. Starr offers private consultations on condo & HOA issues. Visit the "contact" pages on DrJoyceStarr.com and StarrPublications.com.

Special book discounts are available for nonprofit groups and for large orders.

Dr. Joyce Starr